I HATE MY EX-HUSBAND
COLORING BOOK

Join our mailing list to be among

the first to find out about special offers,

discounts and our new releases!

Sign up at:
www.adultcoloringworld.net

@adultcoloringworld

facebook.com/adultcoloringworldbooks

@adultcolorworld

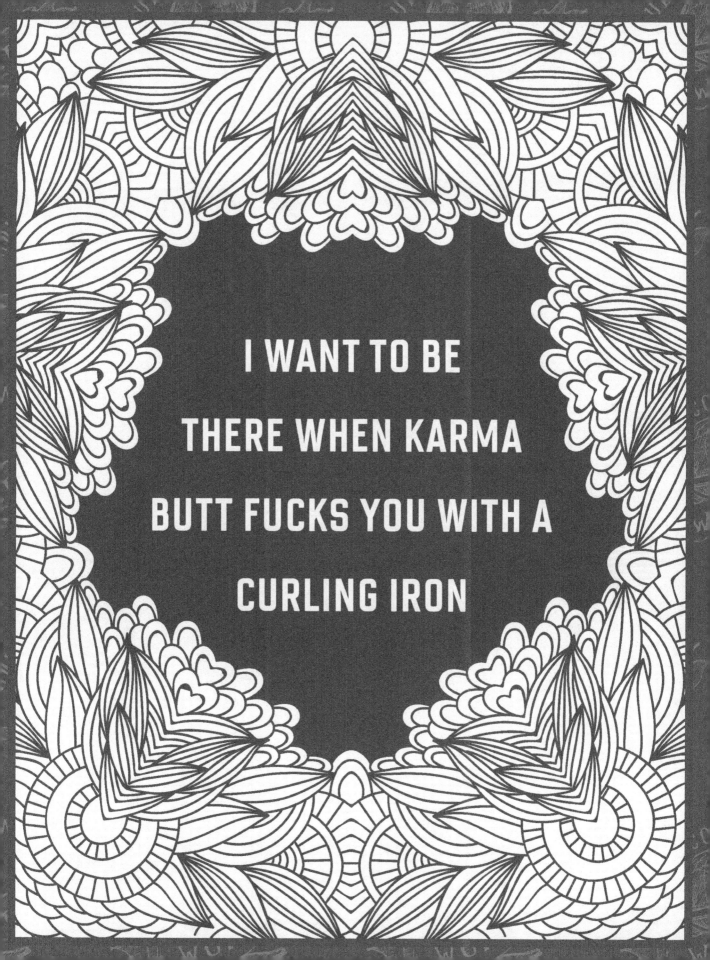

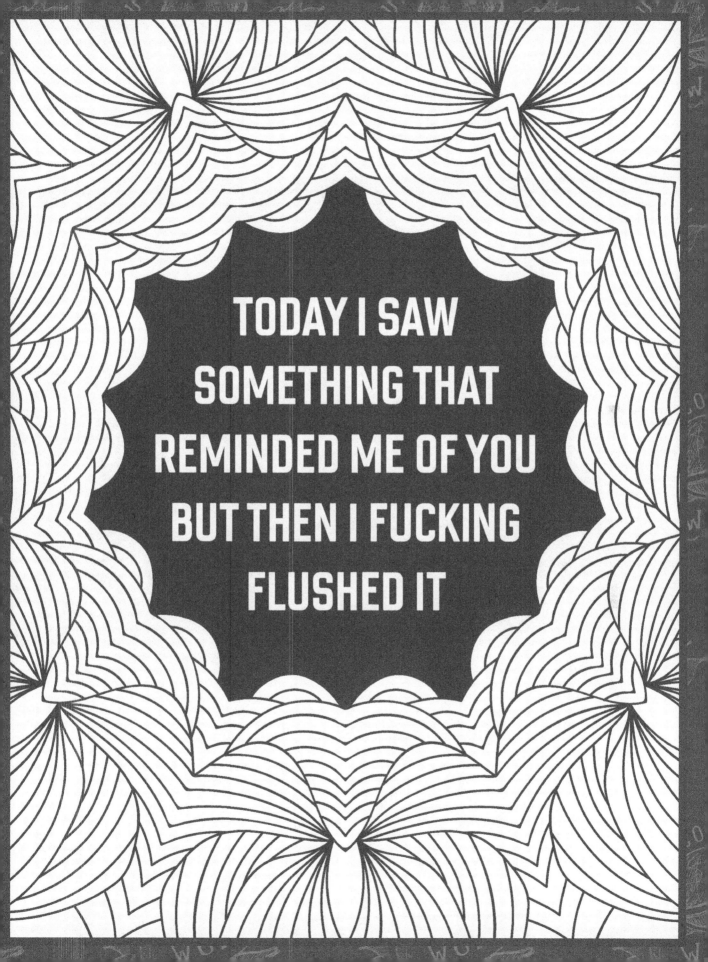

TODAY I SAW SOMETHING THAT REMINDED ME OF YOU BUT THEN I FUCKING FLUSHED IT

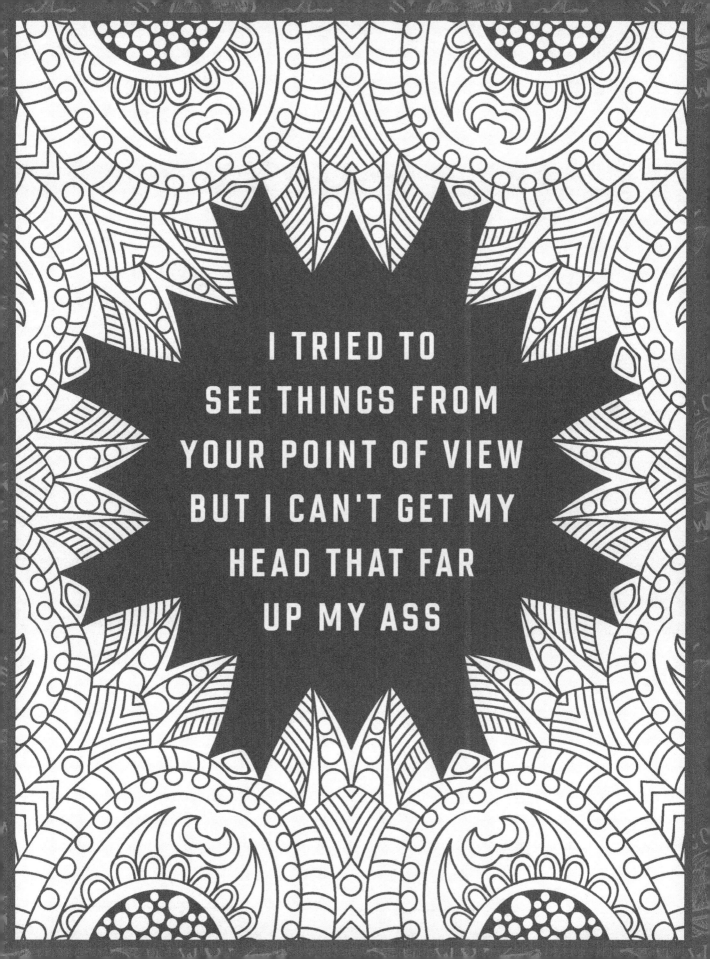

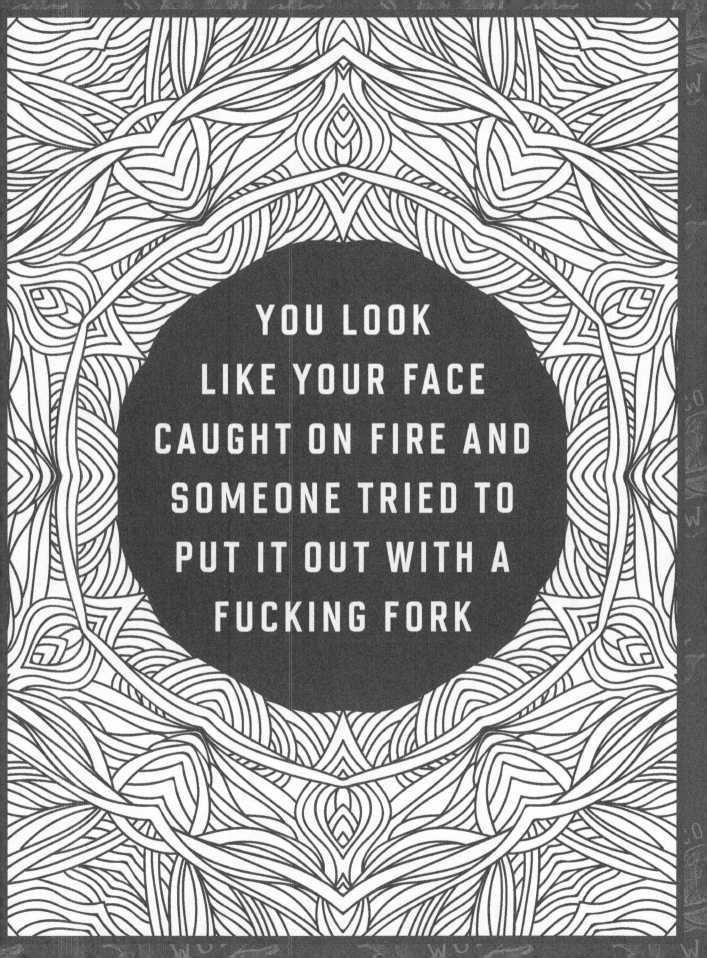

YOU LOOK
LIKE YOUR FACE
CAUGHT ON FIRE AND
SOMEONE TRIED TO
PUT IT OUT WITH A
FUCKING FORK

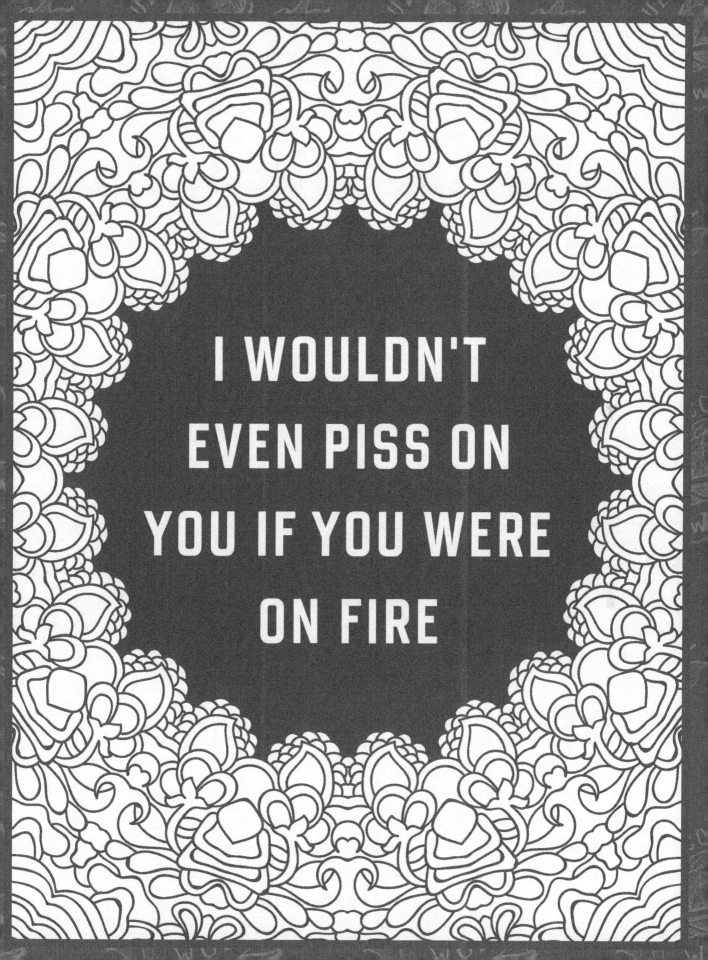

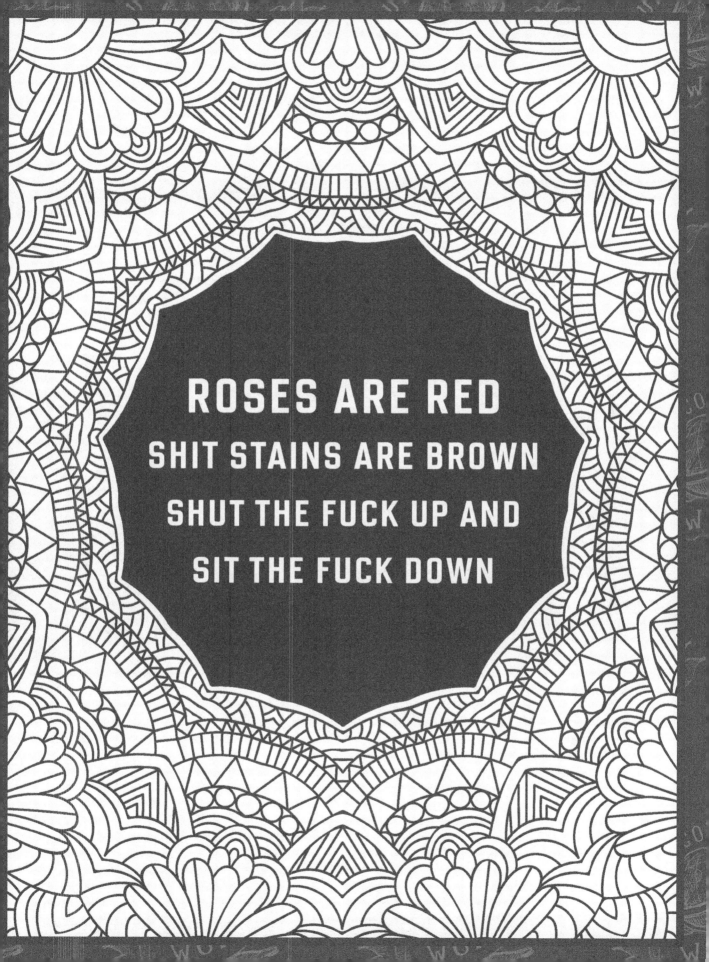

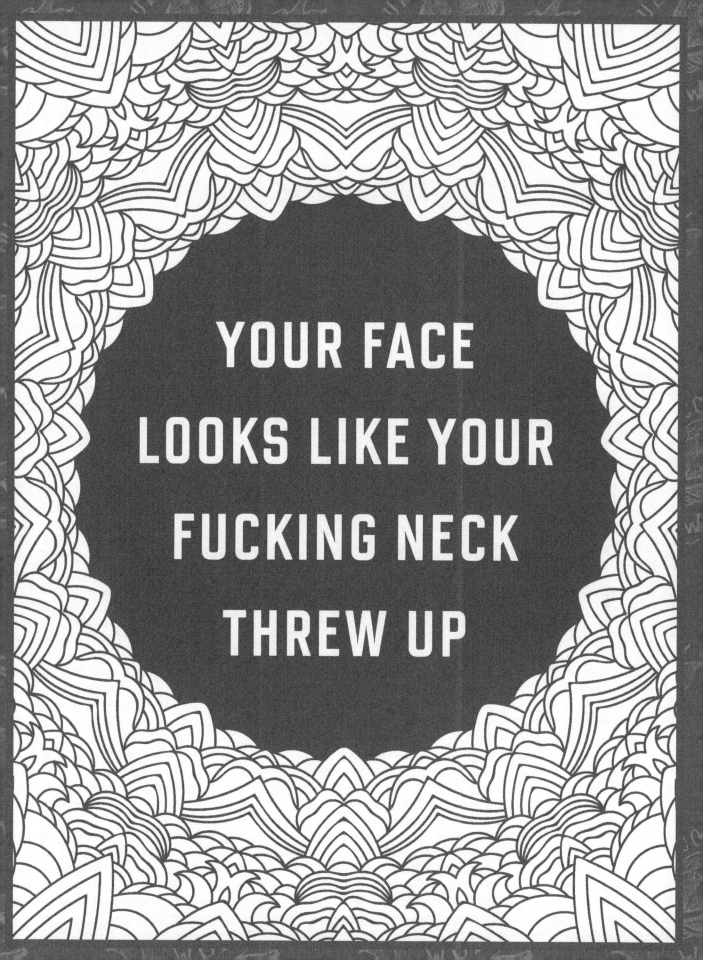

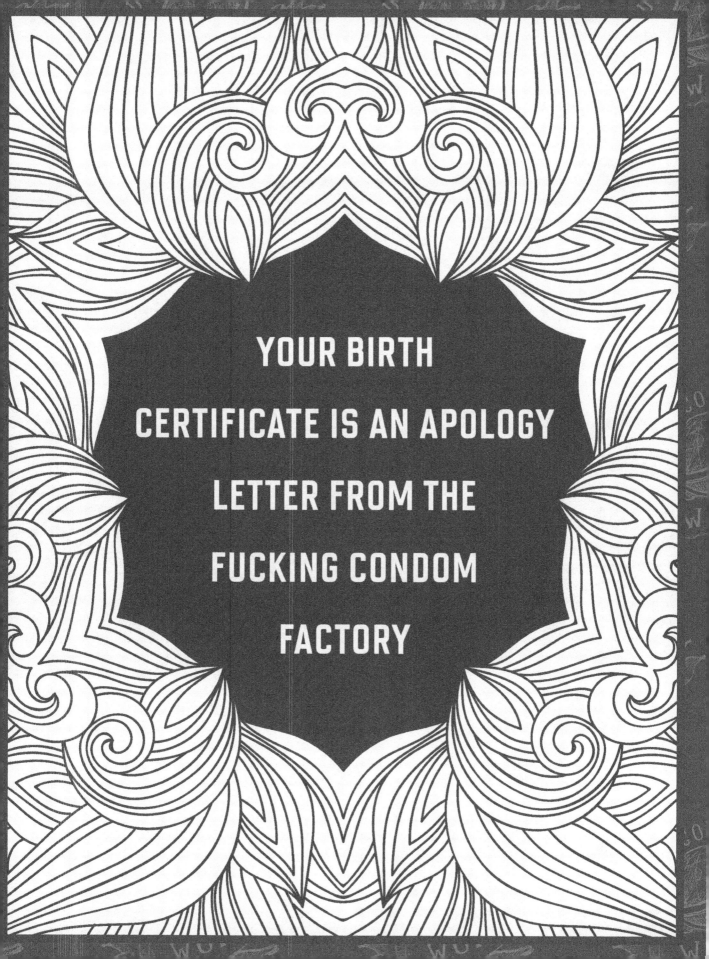

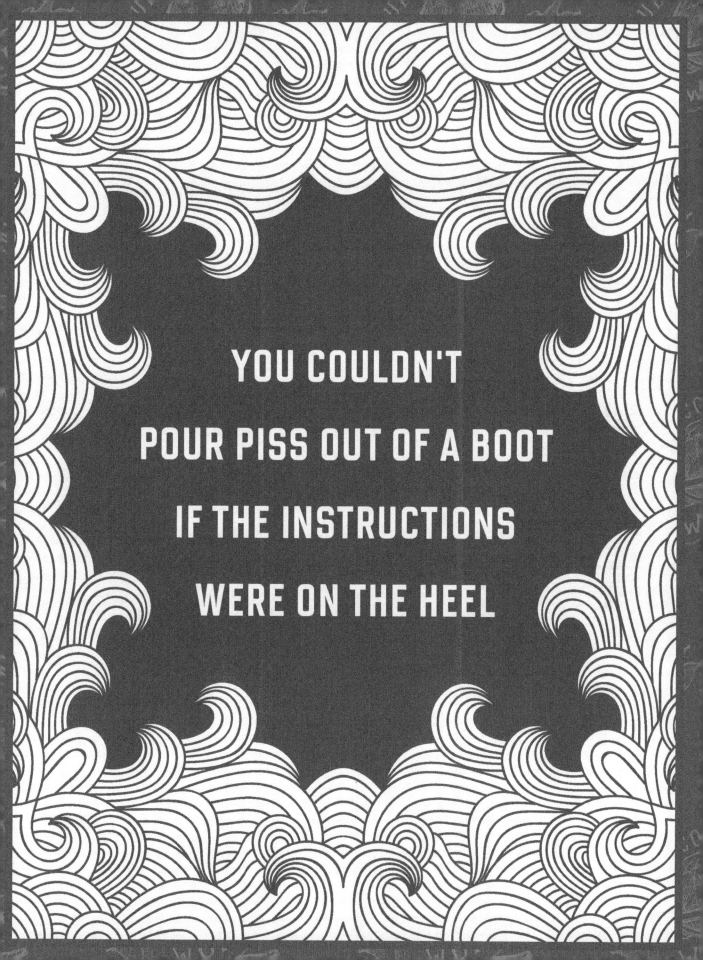

YOU COULDN'T
POUR PISS OUT OF A BOOT
IF THE INSTRUCTIONS
WERE ON THE HEEL

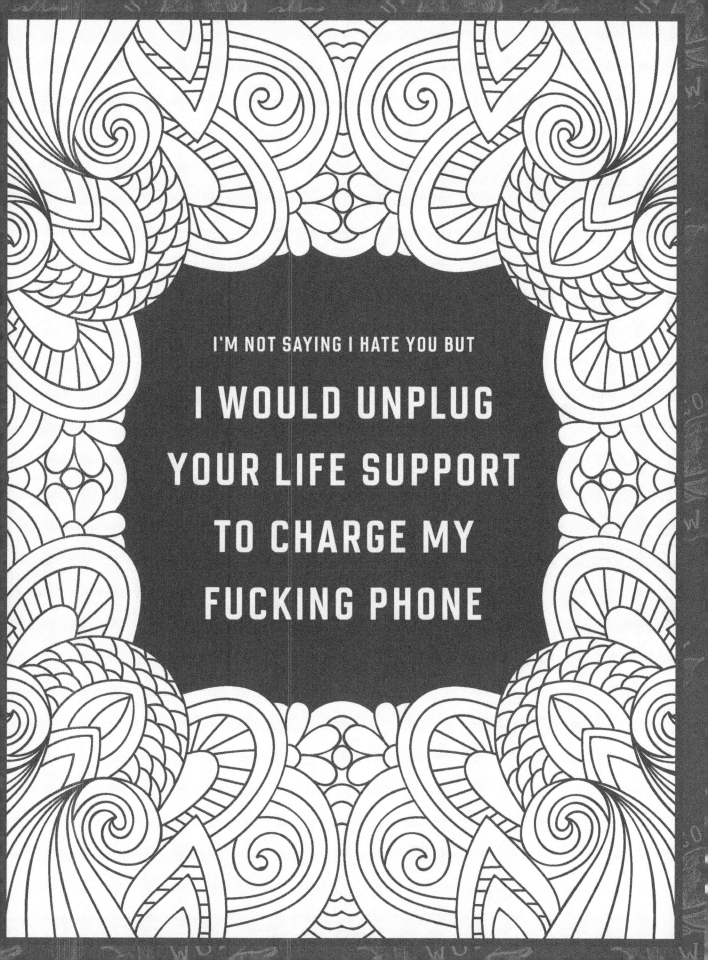

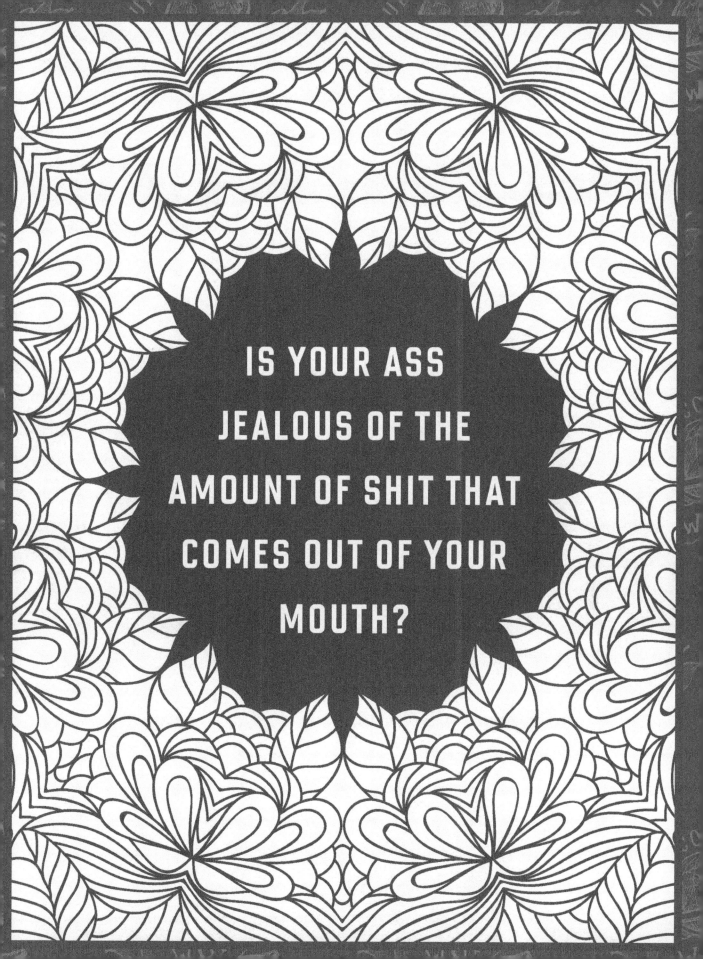

IS YOUR ASS JEALOUS OF THE AMOUNT OF SHIT THAT COMES OUT OF YOUR MOUTH?

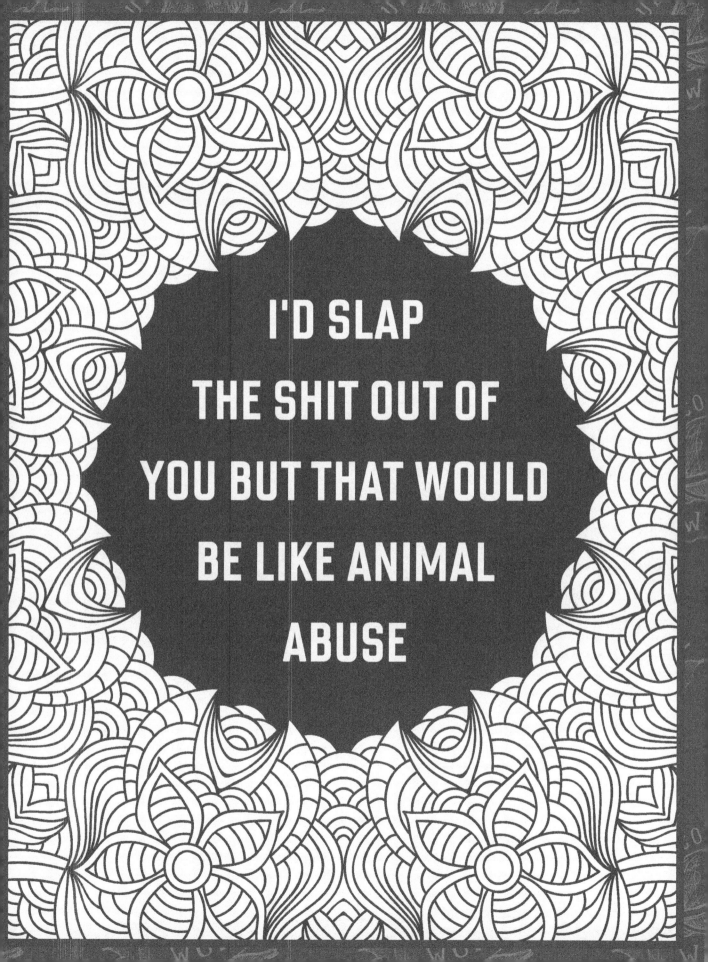

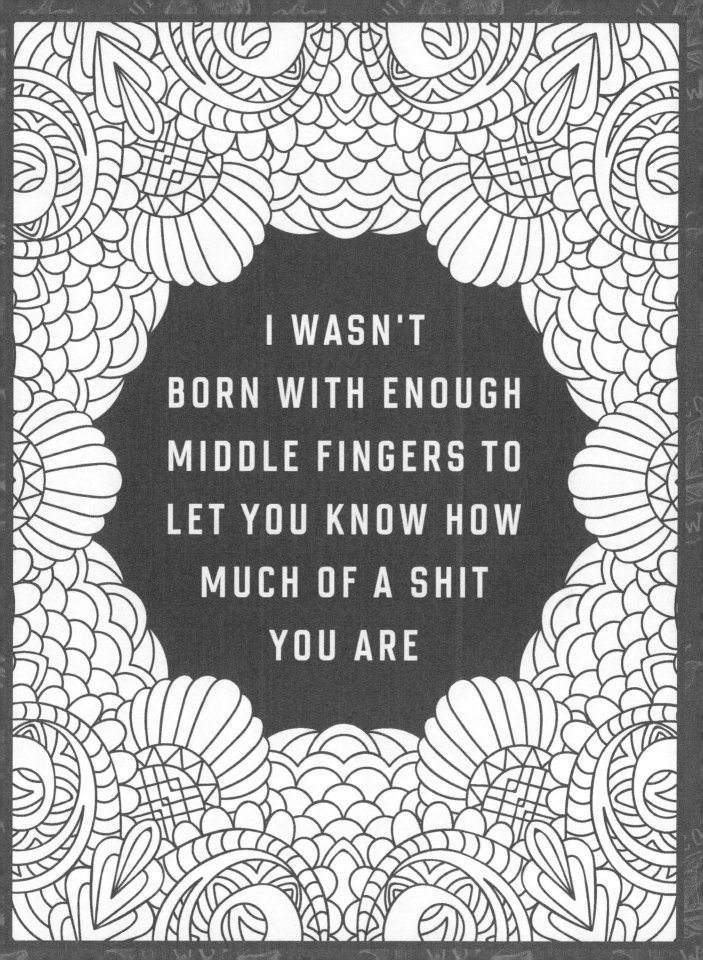

I WASN'T
BORN WITH ENOUGH
MIDDLE FINGERS TO
LET YOU KNOW HOW
MUCH OF A SHIT
YOU ARE

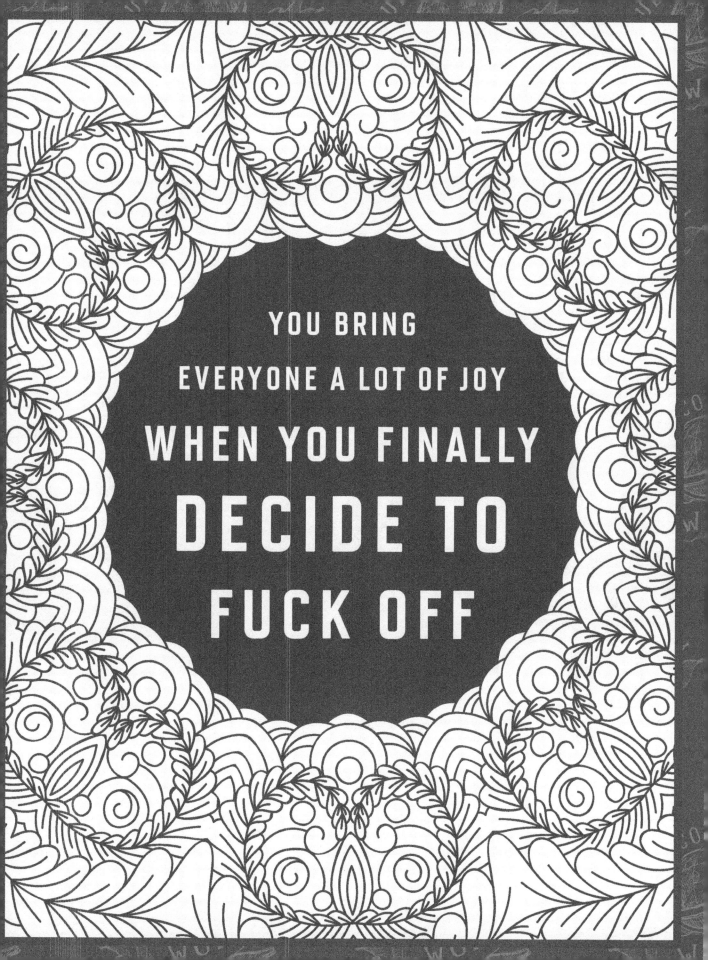

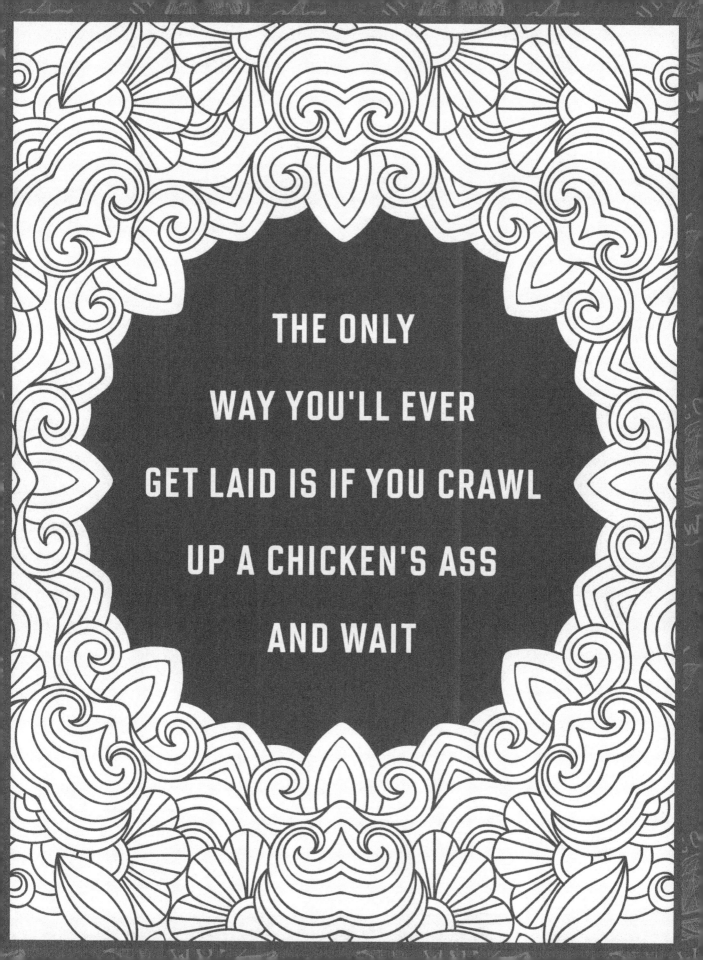

THE ONLY

WAY YOU'LL EVER

GET LAID IS IF YOU CRAWL

UP A CHICKEN'S ASS

AND WAIT

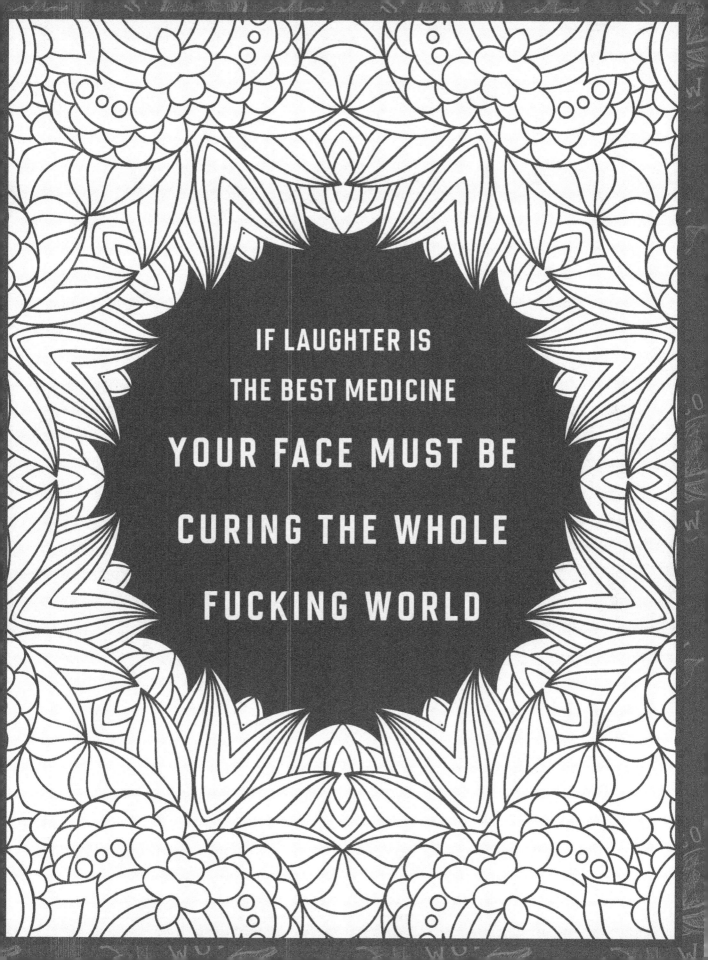

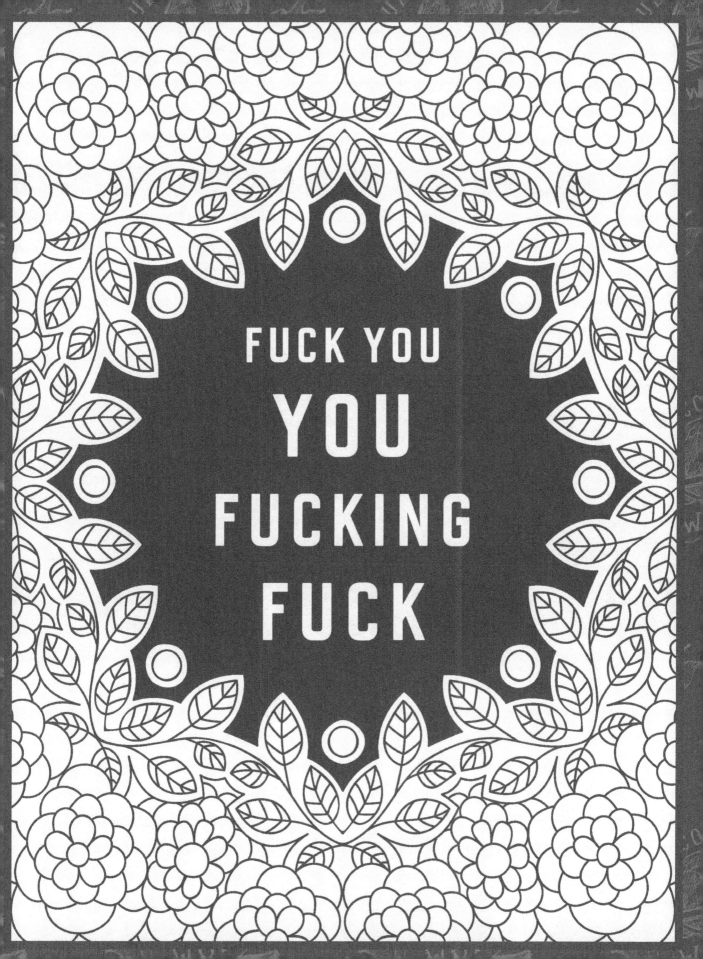

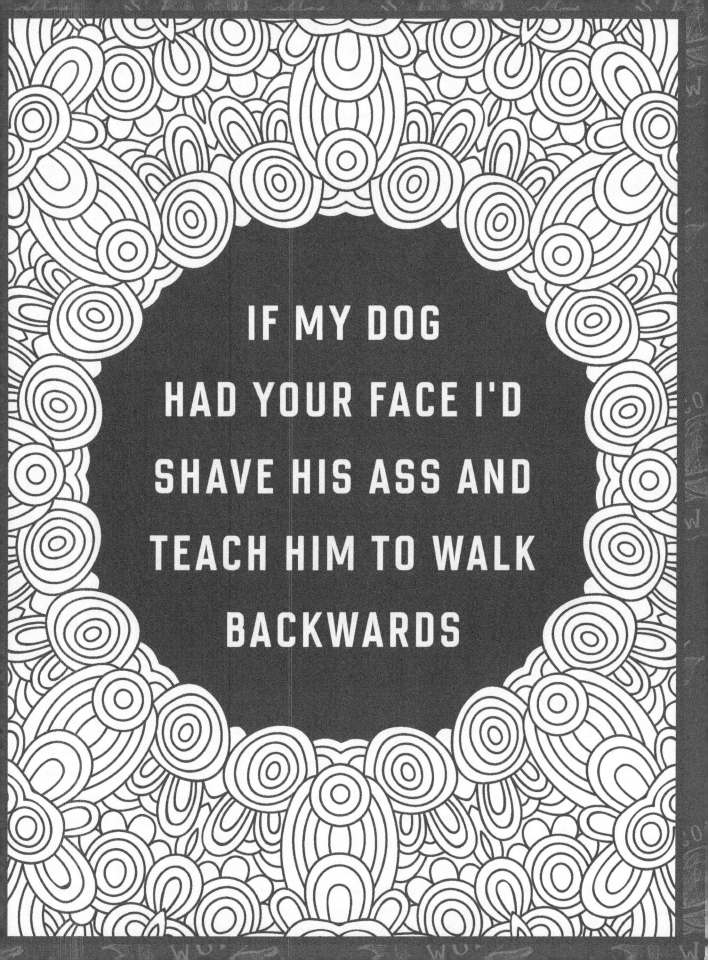

IF MY DOG
HAD YOUR FACE I'D
SHAVE HIS ASS AND
TEACH HIM TO WALK
BACKWARDS

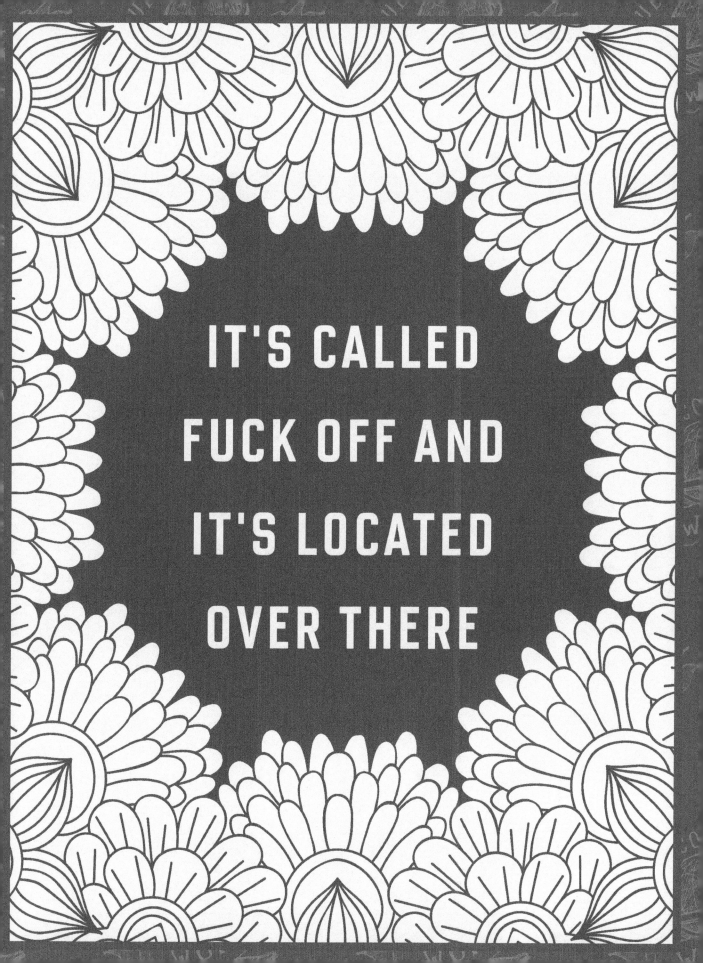

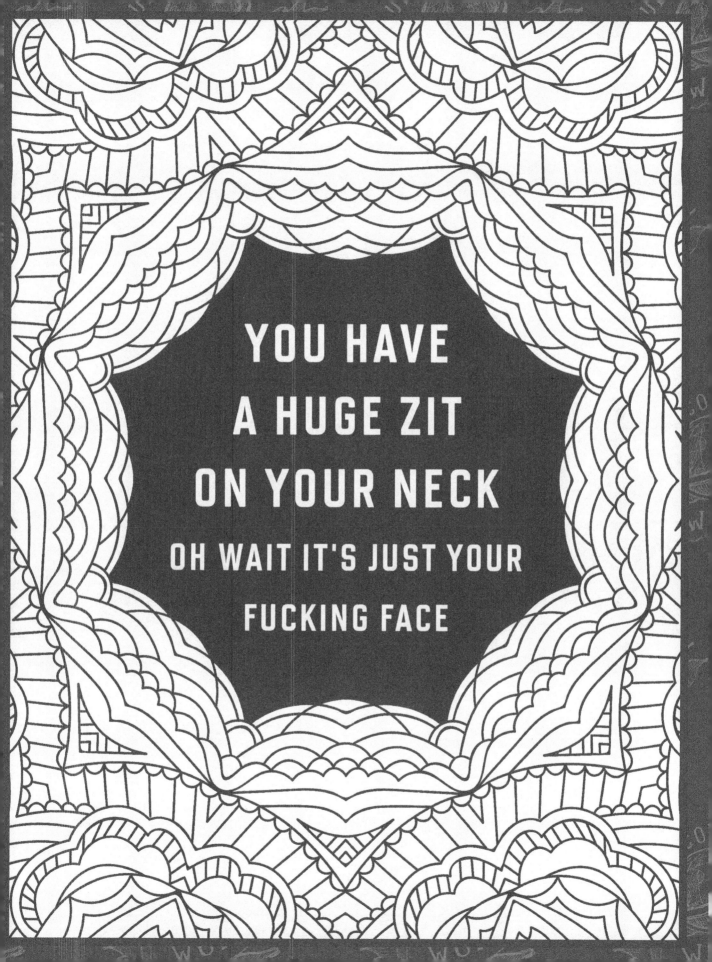

YOU HAVE
A HUGE ZIT
ON YOUR NECK

OH WAIT IT'S JUST YOUR

FUCKING FACE

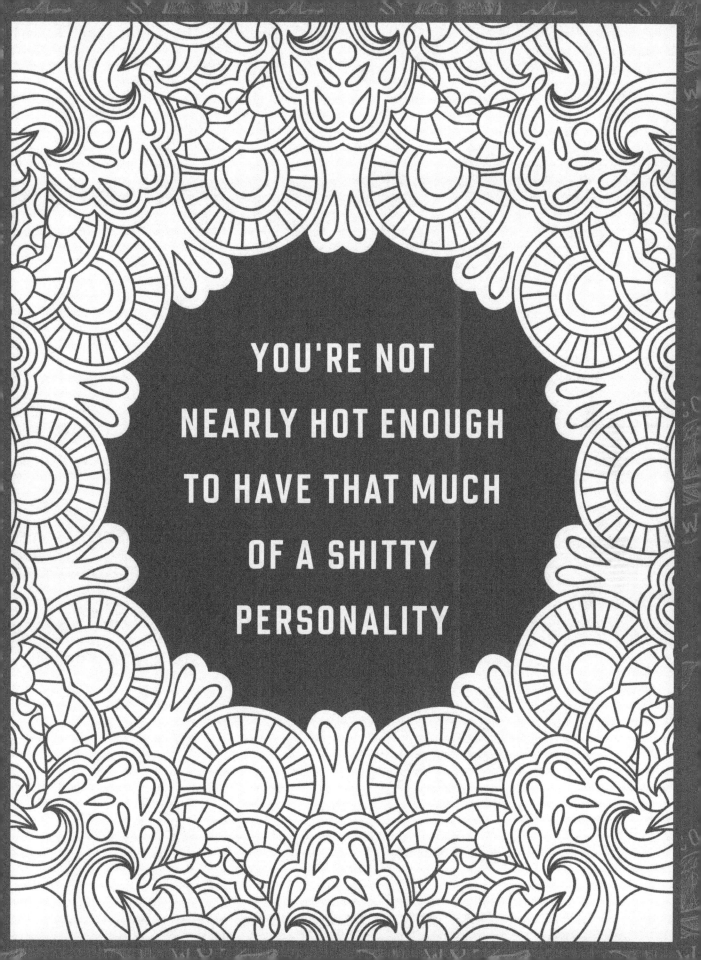

YOU'RE NOT
NEARLY HOT ENOUGH
TO HAVE THAT MUCH
OF A SHITTY
PERSONALITY

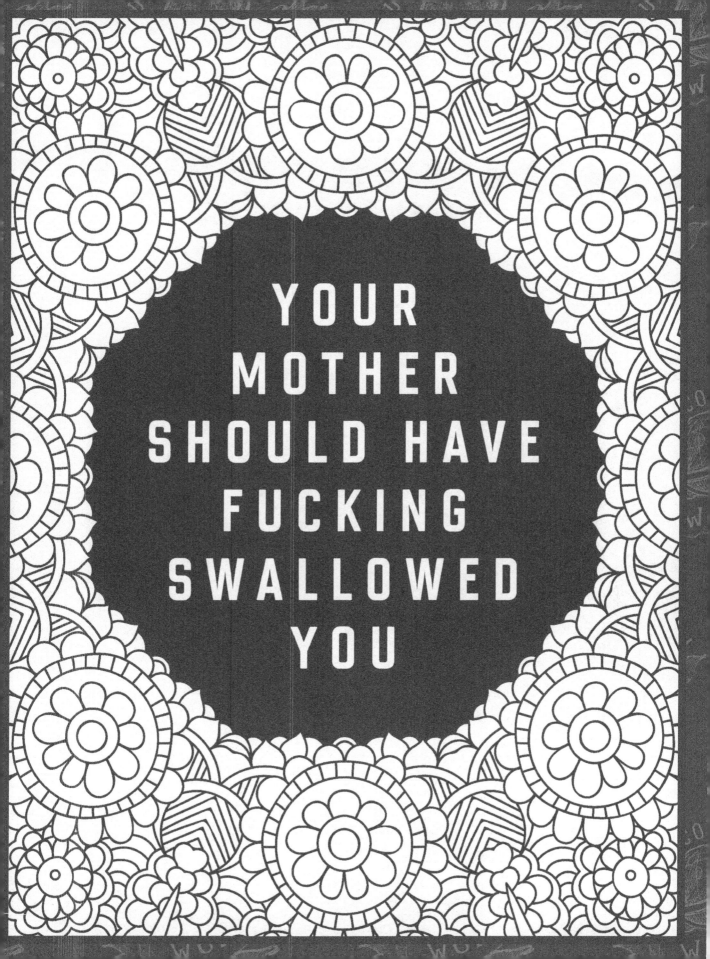

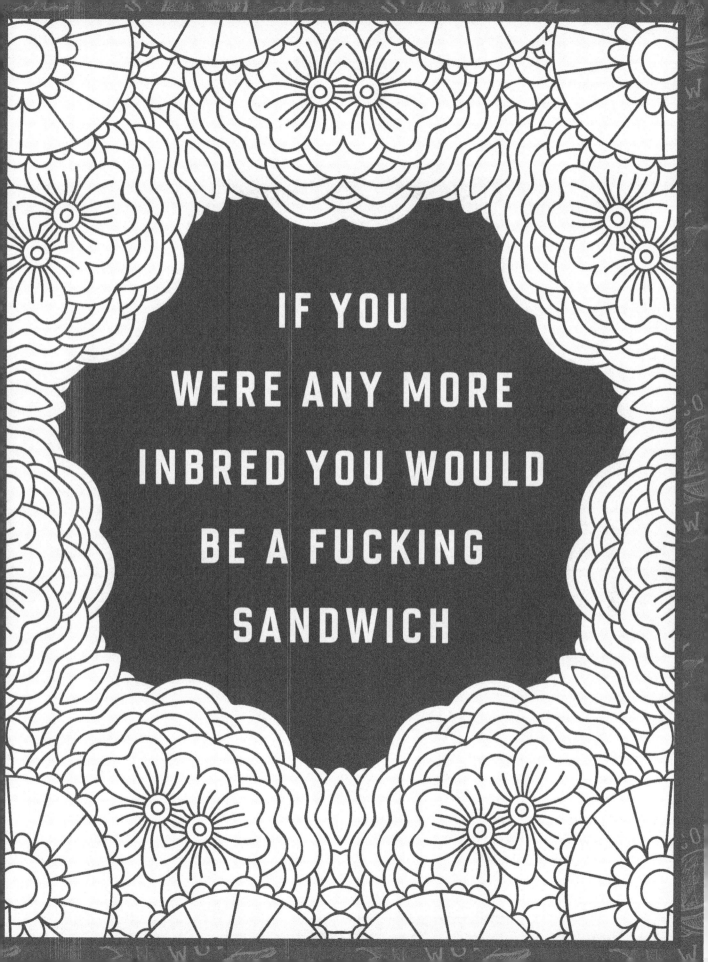

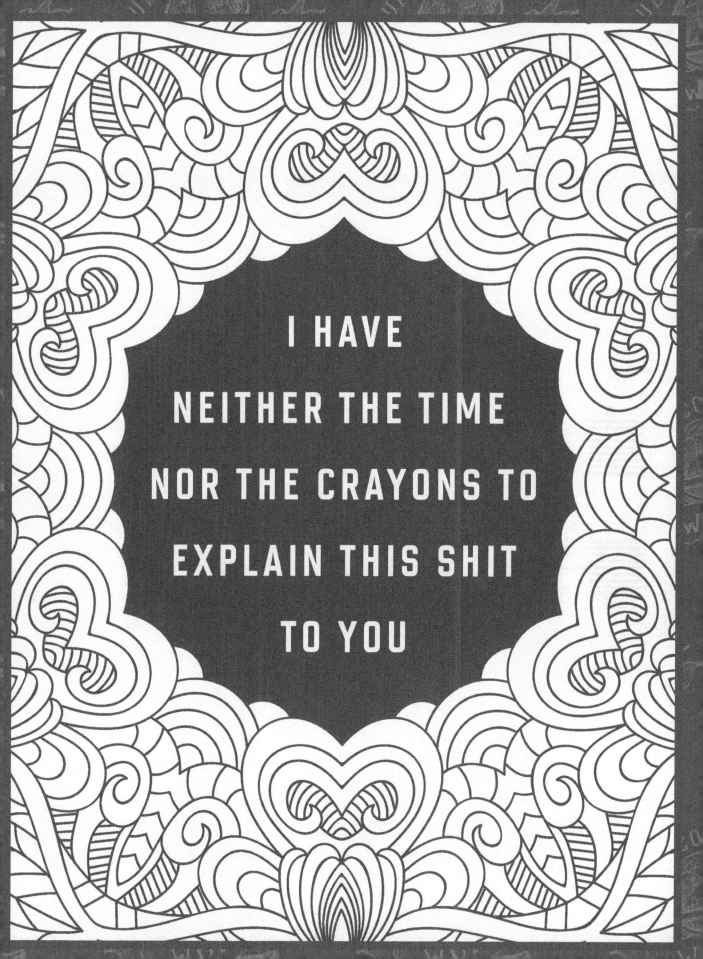

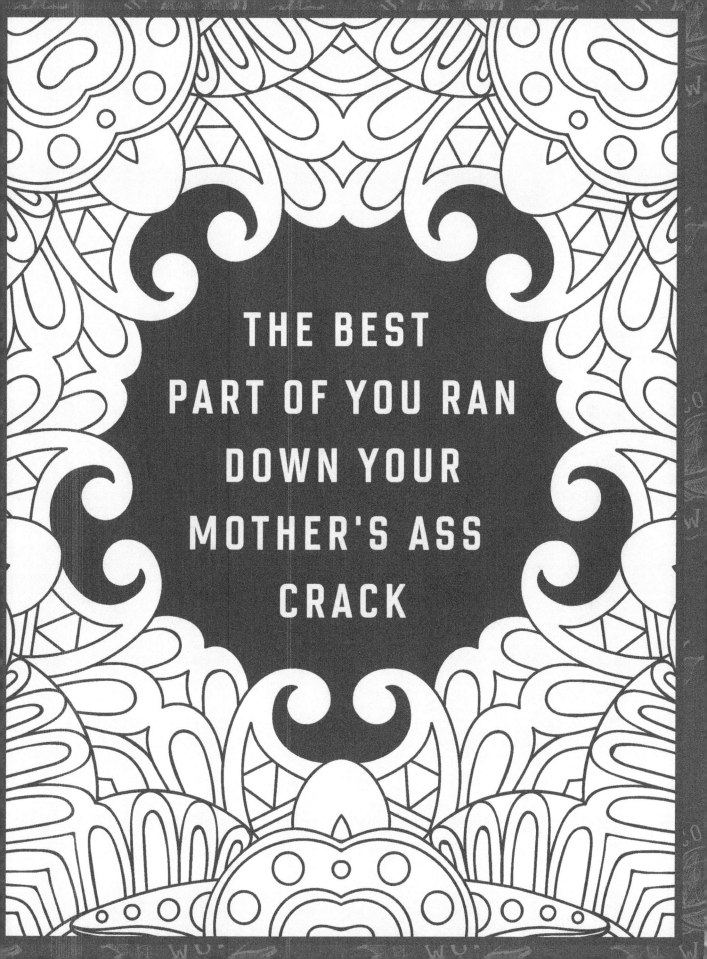

THE BEST
PART OF YOU RAN
DOWN YOUR
MOTHER'S ASS
CRACK

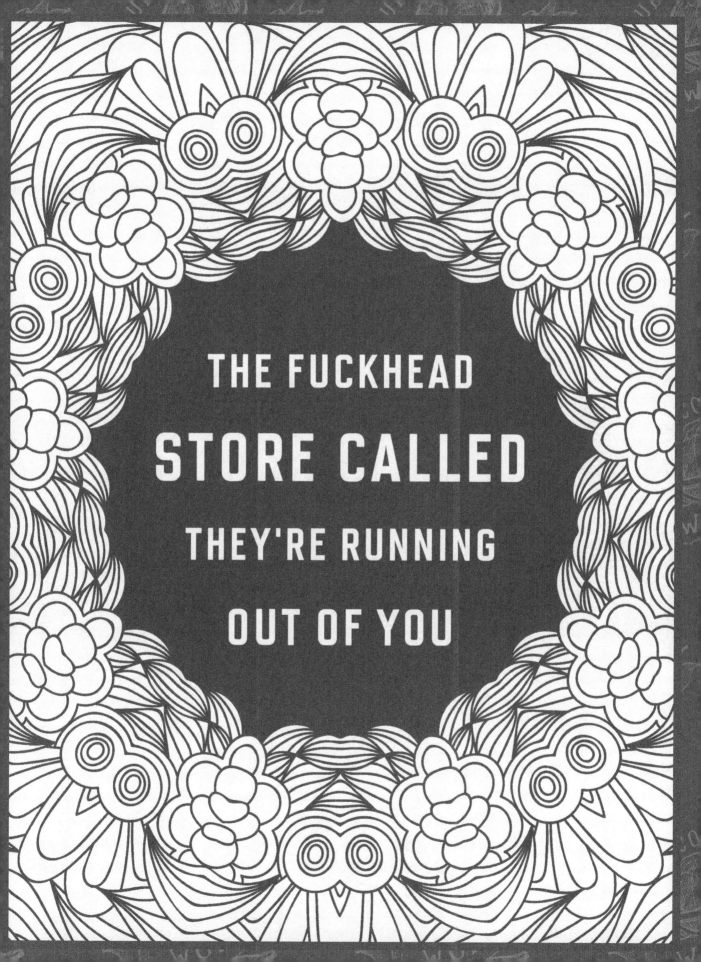

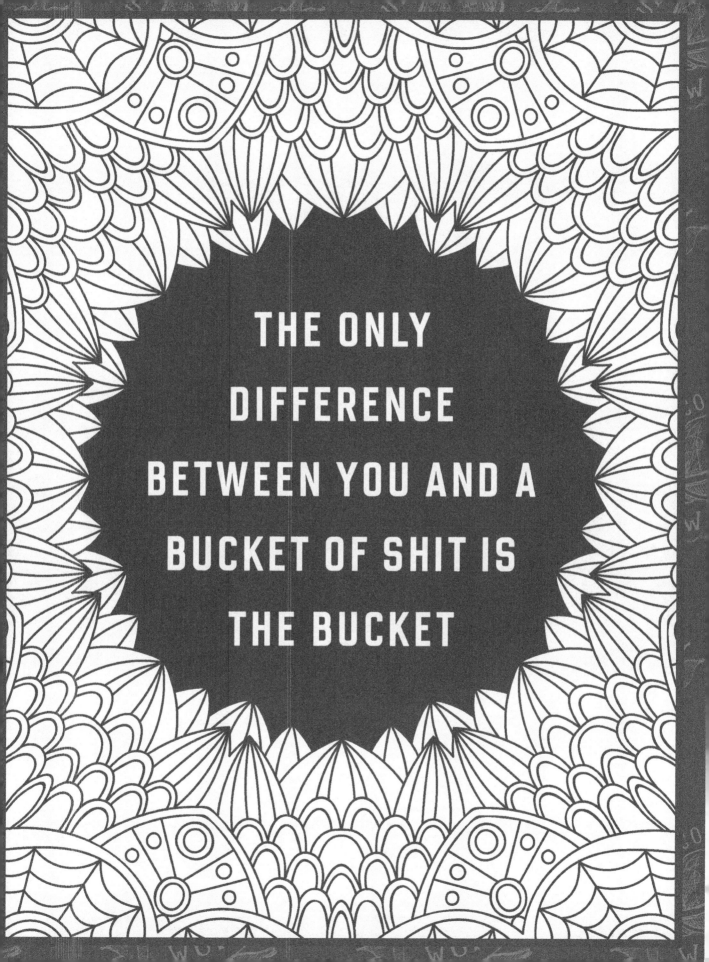

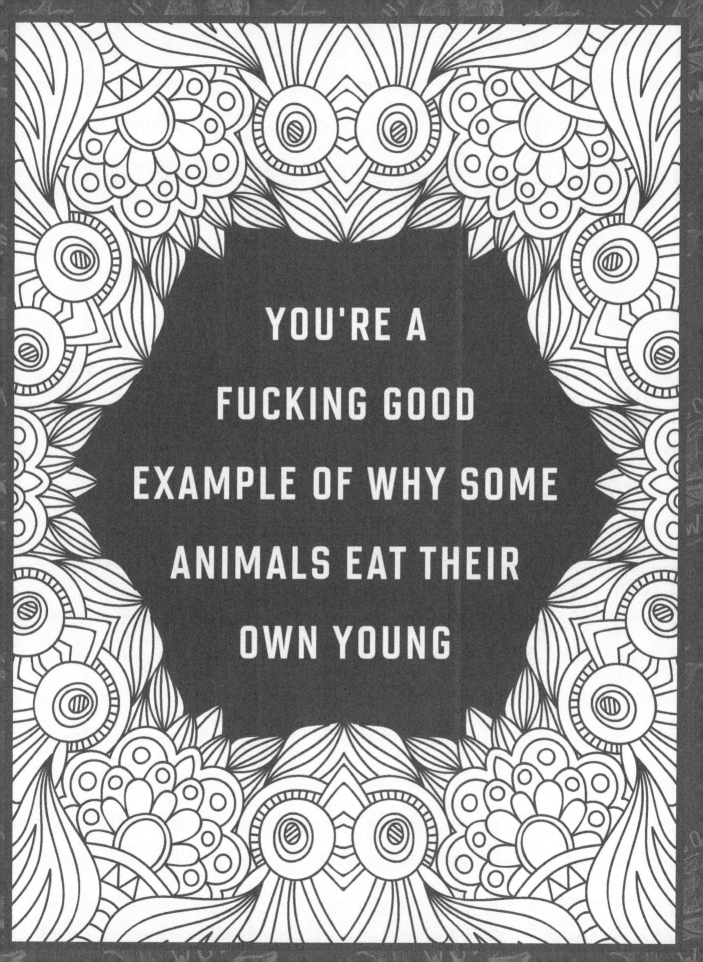

YOU'RE A FUCKING GOOD EXAMPLE OF WHY SOME ANIMALS EAT THEIR OWN YOUNG

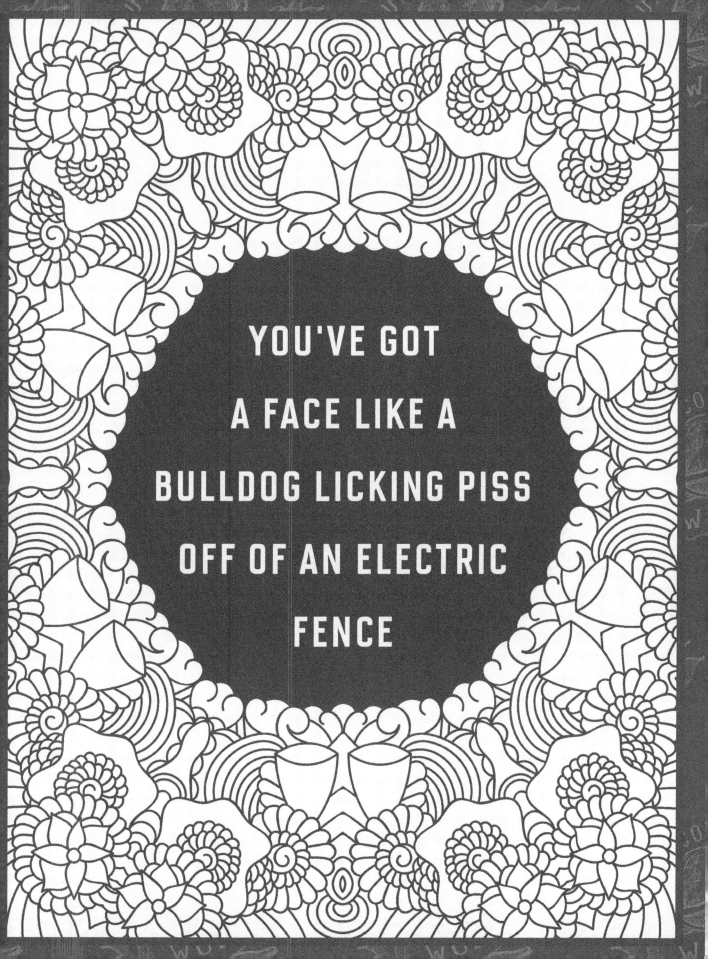

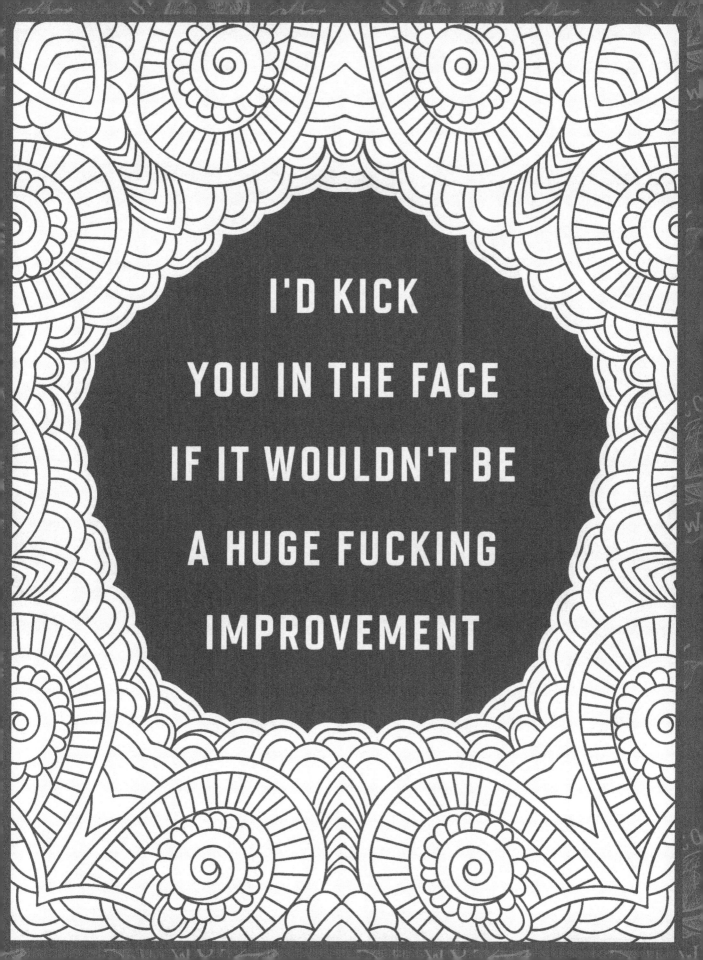

I'D KICK
YOU IN THE FACE
IF IT WOULDN'T BE
A HUGE FUCKING
IMPROVEMENT

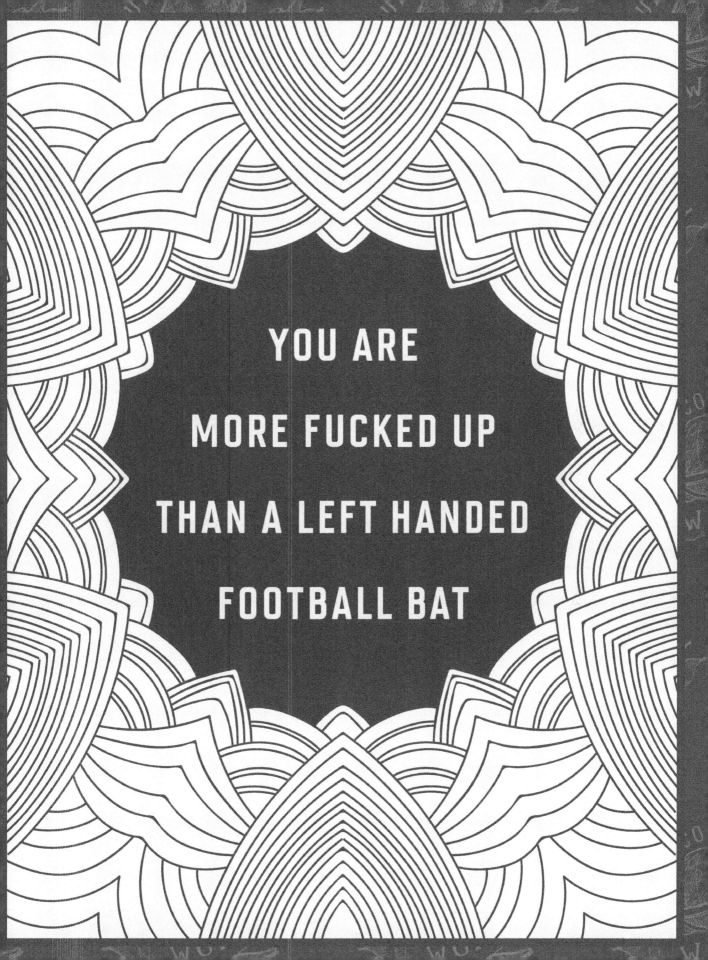

YOU ARE

MORE FUCKED UP

THAN A LEFT HANDED

FOOTBALL BAT

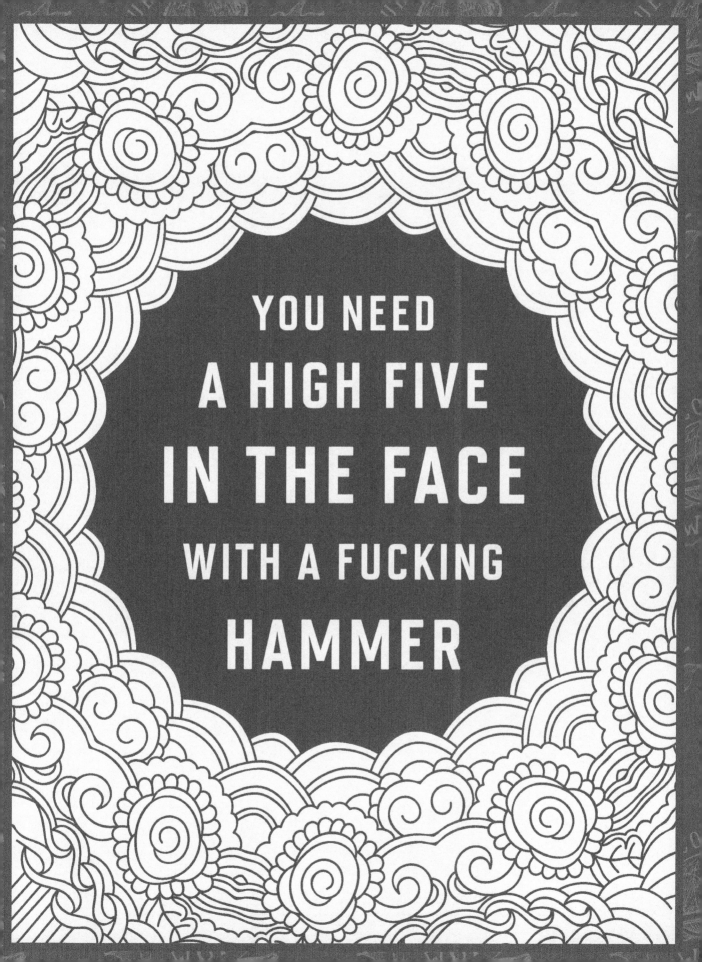

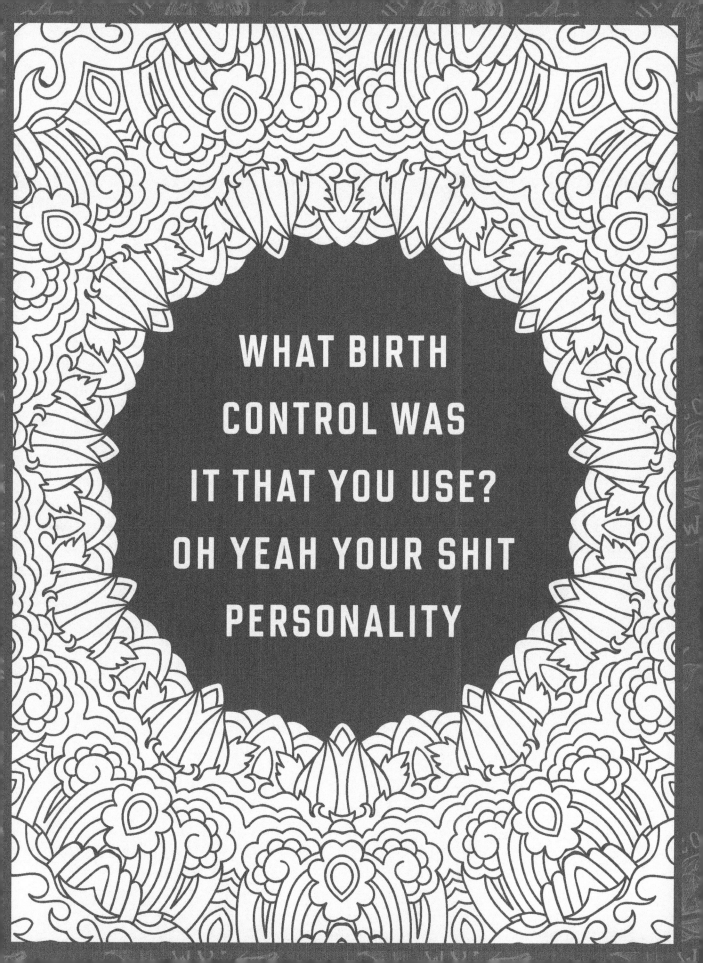

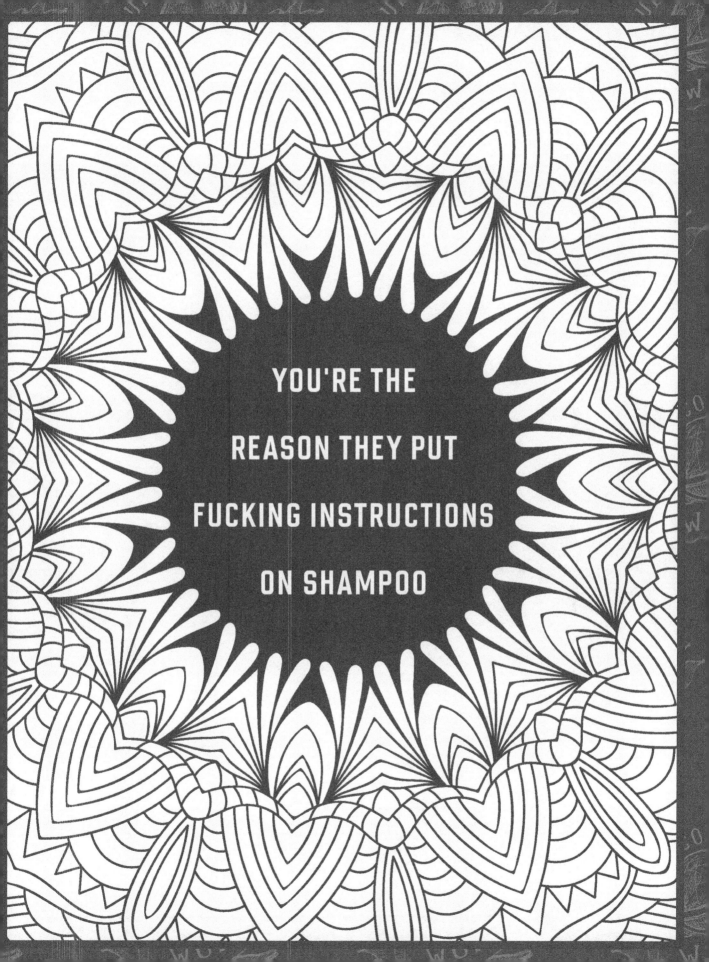

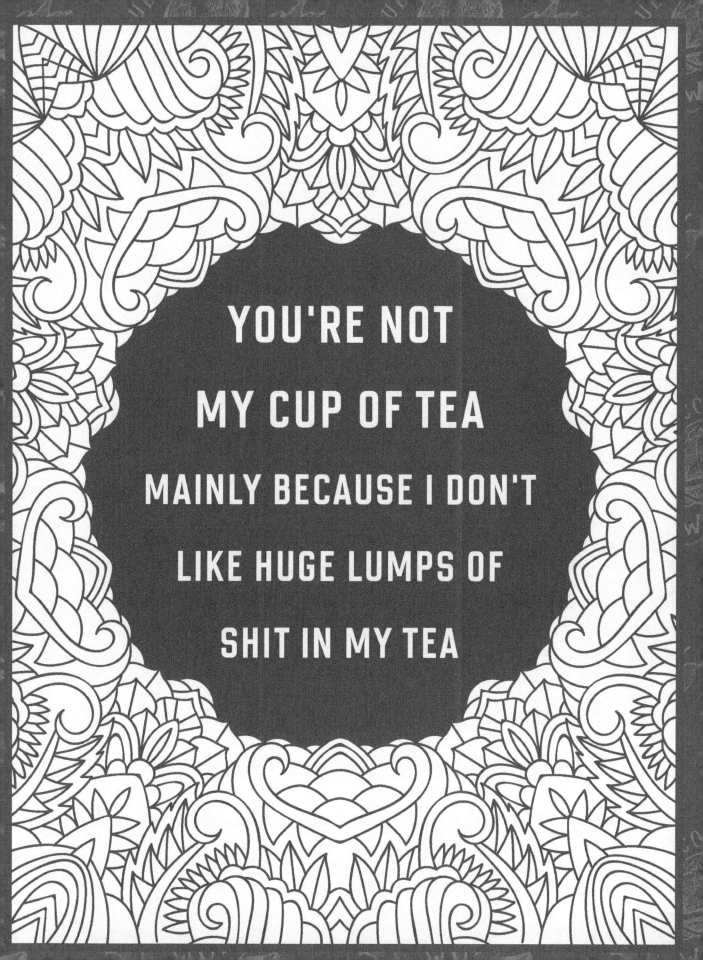

YOU'RE NOT
MY CUP OF TEA
MAINLY BECAUSE I DON'T
LIKE HUGE LUMPS OF
SHIT IN MY TEA

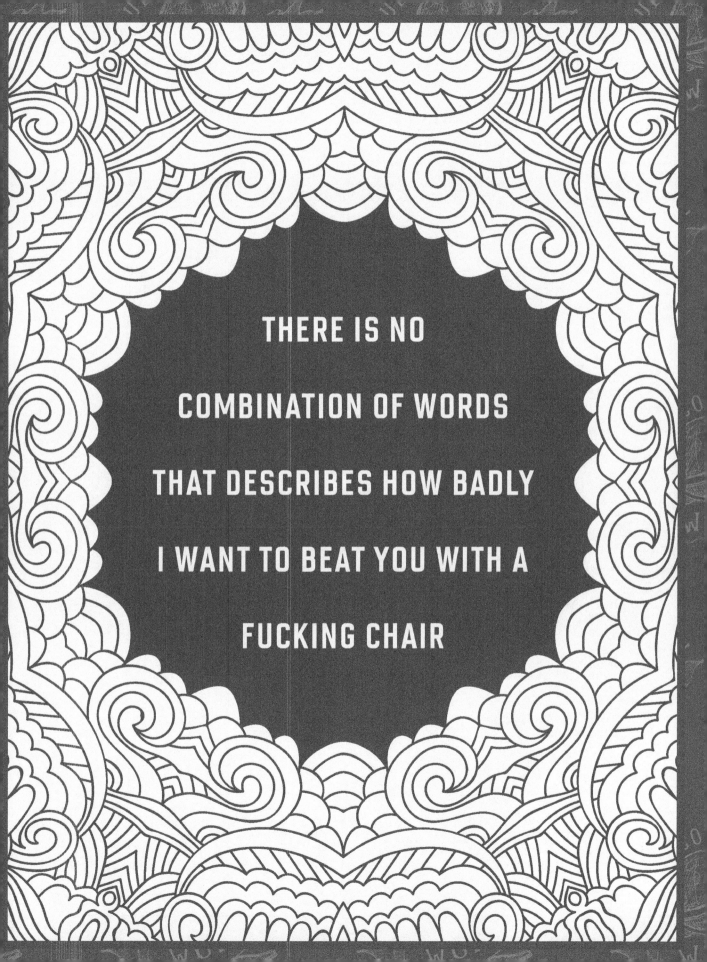

THERE IS NO

COMBINATION OF WORDS

THAT DESCRIBES HOW BADLY

I WANT TO BEAT YOU WITH A

FUCKING CHAIR

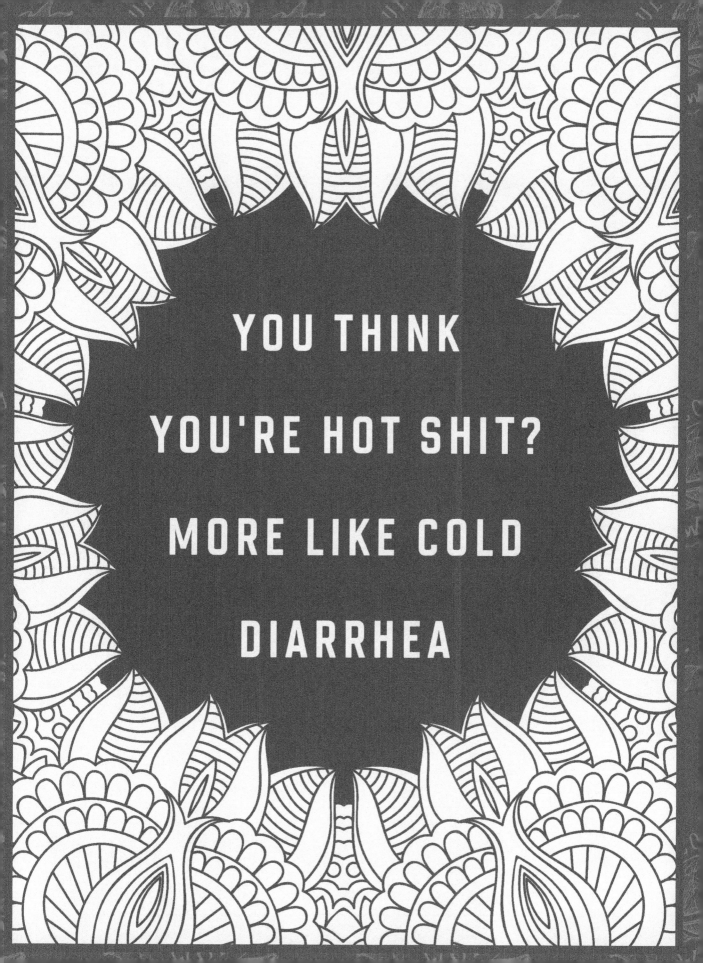

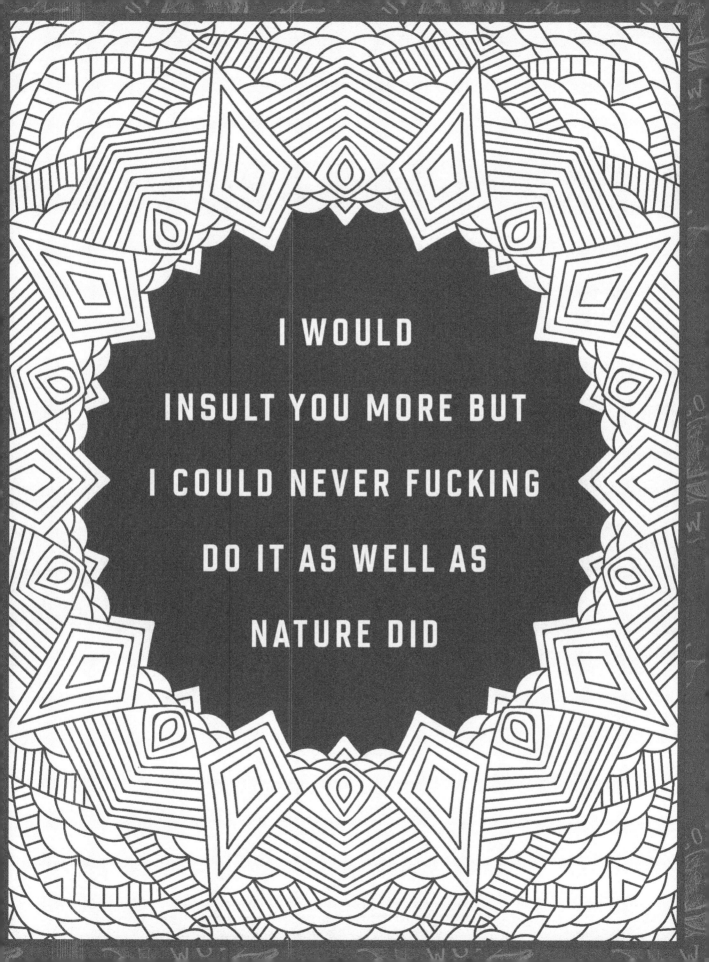

I WOULD
INSULT YOU MORE BUT
I COULD NEVER FUCKING
DO IT AS WELL AS
NATURE DID

COLOR TEST
PAGE

COLOR TEST
PAGE

COLOR TEST
PAGE

WE HOPE YOU ENJOYED THIS BOOK!

TO VIEW OUR HUGE
RANGE OF ADULT COLORING
BOOKS, VISIT OUR WEBSITE
TODAY AND DON'T FORGET
TO FOLLOW US VIA OUR
SOCIAL ACCOUNTS!

ADULTCOLORINGWORLD.NET

📷 @adultcoloringworld

f facebook.com/adultcoloringworldbooks

🐦 @adultcolorworld

Made in the USA
Coppell, TX
29 April 2022

77173279R00050